DODO FEATHERS

ALSO BY JAMEY HECHT

Limousine, Midnight Blue: Fifty Frames from the Zapruder Film

Plato's Symposium: Eros and the Human Predicament

How to Write about Homer

Sophocles' Three Theban Plays: Antigone, Oedipus the Tyrant, Oedipus at Colonus
A Translation with Notes and Commentary

DODO FEATHERS
Poems 1989-2019

JAMEY HECHT

International Psychoanalytic Books (IPBooks)
New York • http://www.IPBooks.net

Published by International Psychoanalytic Books (IPBooks)
Queens, New York
Online at: www.IPBooks.net

Copyright © 2019 Jamey Hecht

All rights reserved. No part of this publication may be reproduced, stored in a retrieval system, or transmitted in any form or by any means, electronic, mechanical, photocopying, recording or otherwise, without the prior written permission from the publisher.

Cover design by Mark Kuzmack of Marksmen Studio.
https://www.marksmen.studio/

Cover illustration by Michael White.
https://www.michaelwhitestudio.com/

Interior book design by Medlar Publishing Solutions Pvt. Ltd., India

www.IPBooks.net

ISBN: 978-1-949093-07-0

To Michael David White

Since my dear soul was mistress of her choice
And could of men distinguish, her election
Hath seal'd thee for herself...
                    Give me that man
That is not passion's slave, and I will wear him
In my heart's core, aye, in my heart of hearts,
As I do thee.
                    —*Hamlet*, III. ii.

What are we coming to?
No room for me, no fun for you...
All the strangers came today,
and it looks as though they're here to stay.

             —*Oh! You Pretty Things* (Bowie)

My thanks to
Joanne Baines, David Benesty, Jennifer Michael Hecht,
Christine Krol, Mark Kuzmack, and Arnold Richards.

Table of Contents

Acknowledgements xi

I

Eclipse 3
Aftermath. 4
First Divorce (*after Lattimore's Homer*) 5
Eighty Million Millennials. 6
1997 in a Nutshell 7
Old Flame 8
Grossman's Tooth. 9
Deathbed Benediction 11
Landscape with Tramp. 13
Twenty Seconds at Surprise Lake Camp in 1986. 15
The Dream of the Welcome Mat 16
Angels, with No Skin in the Game 17
Ticket. 18
Miners Dig Deep. 19
Over But Not Over But Over 20
What's So Ugly 21
Hot January 22
She's Gone, But 23
The Meaning of Life Is the Location of the Universe 24

II

Chariot. 29
Homer's *Iliad*, Book I lines 1–66 30
Homer's *Iliad*, Book IV lines 1–42 33

The Sirens...35
Saving Ajax 38
Polonius' Lament 40
Barnardine 41
Paradise and Hell Lost................................43
Satan's Moods..45
Faustus 46
The Seven Deadly Sins................................47
Mania...48
The Earth Was without Form, and Void 49
"Strong Thunderstorms Result in Deaths of Two" 50

III

The Late Beach.......................................53
The Ride..54
Gloves (or, Night's Hand) 55
Revolving Door 56
Pencil Sharpener.....................................57
Housework...58
Homage to Billy Collins..............................59
Casper the Friendly Ghost............................60
Oscar the Grouch Crosses the Pacific Garbage Patch ...61
Livestock in the Eisenhower Years....................62
Noah..63
The Golem 64
Music...66
Hugo Wolf (Austrian Slovenian composer, 1860–1903) ...67
Aafje Heynis (Dutch contralto, 1924–2015) 68
Maria Callas (Greek American soprano, 1923–1977) 69

IV

Wedding Wagon 73
Problem Solving......................................74
Harmless 75
The Round Square (or, Manifesto of the Left Hemisphere).......76

Tyrannosaurus Rex.................................77
The Razorback....................................79
Eohippus: "Dawn Horse"...........................80
Giant Extinct Camel..............................81
Dying Bee..82
The Death of the Fly.............................83
Fly Killing......................................84
Yeast in a Vat: A Parable........................85
Fido...86
Counterfactual...................................87
Blueberry Swirl (or, Privilege)..................88
Large Big Jumbo..................................89
Richard Nixon at Bosworth Field (1485/1974)......90
1865...92

Acknowledgements

"The Sirens"
Arion, 25.3, Winter 2018.

"Aafje Heynis," "Hugo Wolf," and "Maria Callas"
The Amalgre Review, Issue 4, Winter 2017–2018.

"Mania"
The American Journal of Poetry, Volume 3, Summer 2017.

"Landscape with Tramp"
The Hiram Poetry Review, Issue # 78, Spring 2017.

"Aftermath"
Rattle, No. 58, Winter 2017.

"Tyrannosaurus Rex"
Marsh Hawk Review, November 2009.

"The Earth Was Without Form, and Void" (formerly "Genesis")
Caesura, Spring 2008.

"Grossman's Tooth"
Tikkun, 24.2, March-April 2009.

"First Divorce"
Rattle, No. 29, Summer 2008.

"The Round Square"
Free Inquiry, Vol. 26 No. 6, October/November 2006.

"Fido"
Block Magazine, June 2, 2006.

I

ECLIPSE

A stand of trees still holds the weedy hill
behind the school I went to forty years ago,
their topmost nerves all swaying in the cold
world's breath, that swells their plastic bags.
Tangled twigs are black against the deep
and clouded blue. Third week in November.
Ravens. Ice. Wet Burger King debris.

Earth's shadow slides, a fragment of the night
whose fall has pierced the day. Below me,
worms digest the castings their ancestors made
when I was in fourth grade, Bicentennial
pennants on my new fake Schwinn. The War
in Vietnam had ended hours before
I kicked the ball and saw it hide the Sun
an instant, so we all looked down, and saw
the silent disk of darkness cross the grass:
the flat immortal shadow of the dying solid sphere.

Aftermath
For B.B.H.

That woman you loved, the one you pine for,
She's gone. It's over. The past has swallowed it.
Likely you will never see her pretty face again.
That is all right. Why is that all right? Because
the mountains are flowing away like water
and all things pass away, tangent to eternity.

2016

FIRST DIVORCE (*after Lattimore's Homer*)
For D.A.W.

We live on the flat surface of the world, and compared with a God,
We can do nothing. If the God or the God's divine messenger
Were to come to Manhattan and approach this bench and sit beside me
(there is plenty of space for Him or Her, and there is no rain)
Then I believe I could do something, as a famous singer does great things
Until he disappoints his people, or is killed; or like a preacher
Who works things with his voice, continually greater, till the God
Reaches out and down with hard bereavement and consumes him.

But as it is, my wife, two years ago, left me: I can do nothing.
I quit my job, moved hundreds of miles away and read and wrote;
Looked hard at other people's lives as they tried to do this or that.
I learned from their stories, but the burning of the world goes on.
Now in my speech I call upon the beautiful past, knowing the lines
Come to nothing and are not poetry; that other men and women
Are left every day by their women and men, their vows torn open
Like trash into which the raccoons tear, eager to eat of it,

And they wreck the yard and the sidewalk and disown the mess of it.
When they have eaten their fill they return to the trees and are gone,
And behind them the sorry, noisome garbage scatters on the lovely grass.
Order and peace and abundance and joy are the long work
To which the young aspire in their early strength,
But madness comes, and the spoiling vermin down the streetlamp.
My wife becomes my ex-wife, and all the bridal veil and dress,
The heaped white lilies of the wedding day, somehow dissolve.

Their promise is consumed. We already happened, and are gone.

2001

Eighty Million Millennials

I hate the way millennials are certain
"Not a problem" is the same as *"Yes,*
I'll bring the fork that you just asked me for,
and yes, I noticed the respect in your request

since you were once a waiter in the past,
just as I am now, since I am twenty-three,
and you have been divorced as long as I
have been alive; so yes, I'll bring a fork

and dignity for both of us, before
your wedge of iceberg lettuce comes along,
cold and cloven and alone, like you, Sir."
Then again, I guess my generation

ate the last fish in the sea, clear-cut
the Adirondacks, and let Nestlé steal
the glaciers of Mt. Shasta for a song.
Eighty million people can't be wrong.

1997 IN A NUTSHELL
For D.A.W.

The mezzo who could not be a suburban
faculty wife, I can't blame for choosing
operas over decades with a manic man
who never understood what he was losing.

I set us up (when I had no self-knowledge
and no people skills, just eloquence and sex)
for total failure at that bogus little college
in Vermont. In retrospect, it still checks

out: my story of abandonment and loss.
But it was my fault for believing you,
when you did that great bouquet-toss
and my sisters knew it wasn't true.

In my mind, Lear's Kent—his voice still ringing:
Too old to love a woman for her singing.

Old Flame
For D.A.W.

Suppose you fuck me over really bad.
Twenty years go by. Then, drinks in town.
It's been forever. I've been really sad.
You've remarried, and he's made a down-

payment on a brownstone. Now you ask me
to forgive you, and I say I do. I don't,
though. And I know I don't. But I can see
you really want this from me, and I won't

deprive you of it because one of us, at least,
should have a decent shot at happiness.
You from our youthful vows released
yourself with one phone call. I guess

I've never been the same. My ring. My name.
I'm not your anything. You're my old flame.

Grossman's Tooth

One day Grossman's upper right front tooth fell out.
It was one of four incisors he had used for centuries
To hold his pipe in place while he explained to us
The mysteries of love, death, warfare, poetry and life.
One day he sent me out for Captain Black, the blue bag,
Which puzzled me because I'd only seen him smoke
The Captain's white bag in the past. *This*, he said,
Pointing to the navy plastic-coated paper, *is what
I smoke*. The tooth, the fluid in his lungs, dementia:
Prices he paid for a thousand thousand afternoons
Thoroughly entranced in his tobacco's royal cloud
That filled the corner office, six great walls of cases
Floor to ceiling: Loebs both red and green, Penguins,
FSG, and seven feet of hardback New Directions
Of which he had written five. Across the quad
A manhole in the middle of the path was at all times
Spewing steam, where each absurdly narcissistic boy
Paced over in a greatcoat like the strong old man's,
To see the ghost of water rise and pool about his knees;
To feel like Merlin while one had the chance, reciting
Blake or Shakespeare to the freezing stars, sad envy
Eating at one's insides like a parasite because so far
One had no book, no job, no students, no degree,
While *he* enjoyed, it seemed from further off than Mars,
Grandiosity beyond the dreams of avarice: the suits,
The neckties loose to make the knot look huge; a voice
Like thunder over Minnesota's parched infinity of dust;
An angel's power to explain each letter of the law.
It took them a week to fit him with a new one, so
For seven days the Oracle of God spoke whistling

Sibilants: *Augussstine*, *Wittgenssstein*, and *Yeatsss*.
How we little birds competed for his love! The few
Grad students grown-up-enough to sit it out looked on
Us desperate orphans with a mix of pity and contempt.
What did we want from him? *This is my anointed,*
My only begotten son, in whom I am well pleased.
When the new tooth came it was off-white, like ivory,
Not brightly blank like an actor's nor tawny like his
Genuine other teeth, that hung on in his jaw like trees
Half-rooted in a flooded field, or pilings by the pier
No longer vertical, listing in the tide a million days.
Twenty-two, I wanted the tooth his head had thrown.
I'm forty now. His giant mind is gone. Half of mine
Is back there in the steam, still searching for the tooth.

2008

Deathbed Benediction
In Memoriam: Allen Grossman, 1932–2014

I hate you, kid. You're 43. We haven't met in decades
Since at 22 you were so stupid as to love my mistress
As your new best friend, and the Department all assumed
You two were fucking for a year. "They're thick as thieves."
You didn't see your PhD go up in flames, yourself changed
from a peregrine (so nearly fledged! so sure to ride
a rising thermal to the summit of Mount Grandiose,
and roost in ease above a sleepy town; rip rabbits into strips
to feed to hatchlings; eyes like Hubble's, wings like mine)
into a lame and sweetly stinking mule with twitching ears.
Lame mule, that walked a thousand miles to wind up here
beside my bed, where the pitiless normal rain of cosmic rays
has overcome my brain's exhausted troops, and perforates
the galleries and hallways of my giant mind: protons crash
through cell walls, close to lightspeed, morning, noon,
all night, like bullets through a grand chateau in 1945,
Belgian, with a burning grove of apples, empty stables, coal,
Louis XIV windows, thinner at the top due to the viscous flow
of glass, that moves like water for a God, while motionless for us,
so slow we're old before we know it's changed: unless the hail
of shrapnel, flak, a million mindless rounds in lead,
interchangeable like my new friends the gamma rays,
each bitter puff of mathematics just like all the rest (if
bullets or these particles could talk, they'd say: *hello goodbye*)
makes change too fast, makes ancient casements fail,
makes old glass speak a single syllable of pain, or makes
my broken neurons vomit out their plans; their precious slime;
the Hebrew, Latin, German I so labored to install; the tomes
of poetry I memorized; my nuanced love of Rilke; God,
about Whose sacred throne I said so many old new things,

goodbye. O mule, the days when I adored you now are gone
forever, to the dark side of the moon. *Jamey*, I once told you,
you are really dim about some things, and you were stumped.
I told you that in private. Yet once I told a crowded hall:
*Jamey, you always say something useful. I can't remember
when you didn't.* Now here's the Third Millennium A.D.
where widows live; where wise men die; where frogs
grow extra limbs, flesh toxic to the egret and the rats;
and SCOTUS picks the President. Your First Lady, one
Katrina, eats Louisiana for a midnight snack. I'm gone.
The jar of witch's salve that can restore your human form
and give you tenure, you still cannot find. It's empty.
Come closer to my bed. O kid! O pretty mule, I go now.
My contempt remains. Yet here's a final fiction, merciful:
You are my heir. It's you I choose, and not my famous sons;
you, and not the daughter with my genius and my eyes.
It's you, my brilliant moron, *senex puer*, king of fools.
A million tears in twenty years in thirteen schools.

2011

Landscape with Tramp

On one side of the weedy trough where train tracks sleep
Sunken six feet down and nailed with eight-inch spikes
Into the floor of God's old "dry" Upstate New York,
A parking lot retards the trees, whose slow and silent

War against the asphalt's fallen wall of darkness goes
Unnoticed by the drivers of these Pacers, Gremlins,
Saabs, a hundred twenty thousand miles odometered,
But still up here in Hicksville, Pop. 667. If one guy dies,

Or moves down to the Bronx to drive a cab, the Devil
May appear in hat and threadbare cutaway tuxedo
Sitting in a burned-out dining car whose ribs, exposed,
Make prison bars of sunshine on the desiccated grass.

This is the Water-Level Line, that died in 1968,
Around the time the busboy held the broken Senator,
His head, whose blood and Aeschylus flowed out
Through grates and drain-pipes, copper, iron, lead,

That bore his spirit through the sewers to the sea.
Built in 1853, the New York Central lived to age 117.
Slaves once watched it pass while glossy crickets
Sprang into the sky, and feral dogs ran from the noise

While kids threw clods that burst against a cattle car.
On one side thrives wheat's useless distant cousin,
Measuring the wind; but opposite, beyond the tracks'
Unnatural riverbed where motes and gnats, black flies,

Mosquitoes, ride on currents of the helpless air,
The parking lot (it's early June, but Fahrenheit 117)
Awaits the mercy of the starlight's cool caress.
Nobody's here, until the six-hundred sixty-seventh man,

Horatio (*a piece of him*), comes barefoot to the bank
With bourbon and a fishing rod, no line at all, sits
Dangling his birthday legs and singing the *McDonald's*
1970's commercials with a dripping smile, not dead yet.

Two towns away, an empty church of fiberglass
Is clad in purple futuristic knobs (some architect's idea,
That quickly lost its role and turned embarrassing).
There is the water tower, a day-glow rainbow on its brow.

There is the maple, split by lightning when the tramp was nine.
He saw it strike. Late afternoon, the thunderstorm alive,
Gigantic like the storm that stabbed and stabbed at Martin
Luther's heart until the fear of Dad subdued him, rain

Heaving and fading, heaving again, when the white bolt
Drove a rod of cinders down the maple's throat, spit ashes,
Sparks, a birdlike yellow flame that flashed and disappeared,
And one brief hand of smoke that spread away forever.

2008

Twenty Seconds at Surprise Lake Camp in 1986

If all life comes from love, and mine is gone,
how will I survive until the future comes?
At camp, I saw a doe step with her fawn
up to the edge of the woods. The air hums

with bees when I go back there in my mind.
The deer are peering from between the trees
and I'm eighteen again, my head full of blind
ambition, Gandalf, Bowie. At our ease,

we three on our ten legs stand as one,
like I was Bambi's Dad; my antlers up,
prepared to charge at any bastard with a gun
who should appear. I love the sun. I cup

my hand behind my ear, and listen hard:
our fawn is breathing. I fall forward.

The Dream of the Welcome Mat

I dreamed: there was a tower on my street
that burned all night, when lightning shot the bell.
I had a twin, demented, furious;
he threw his clothes into the flames.
Up from the burning bell he rose,
sweat-bright and fat.
He fell ten days from heaven to the floor
and landed by the welcome mat that said:
Every day is new. It isn't true.

Angels, with No Skin in the Game

I guess the angels, with no skin in the game,
regard our lives (our loves gone wrong,
our childless midlife Christmases in jail,
our dear demented mothers on the floor)

as well-turned stories with a tragic arc
like those cathedral doors they watched
us build for them before we learned to fly
in our tin pods from Houston to the Moon.

I guess the angels read our lives like tales
to pass the afternoon; threescore and ten
years are one angelic hour in the sun.
What we live, they watch from elsewhere,

as we watched the face of Marlon Brando
melt: Marc Antony one minute, Colonel
Kurtz the next. We saw the patsy shot
at his arraignment. That's entertainment.

Ticket

Admit one. Whoever holds this passes
to the Night's own home, where grow
wild spores of thought, adrift no more.
Below dead cables on the ocean floor,
past walls of bottles in repose, you go
into the cave of making, where the ceiling,
when some match or glowing insect cracks
the dark, shines wet. Your ticket's red.
So is the room where Truth lies, naked
on her bed, alive and female, smoking
time in long cool drags. But no one's there
to tear your ticket, nod, and let you in.
Your mind has ended, waiting to begin.

Miners Dig Deep
For Dahlia Nissan Russ

Miners dig deep, but for just one thing.
It doesn't matter if it's coal, or gold.
They sell the boss their labor, bring
their wages home. What they dig is sold

abroad, by who-knows-who. For free,
they hand it over to the Man. They give
him all the Earth gives them. They see
him turn it into yachts and coke, live

like a king. They choke on coal dust
in the shafts. Damp darkness for them,
and hot arc lamps. They must trust
miles of metal cable, and a tiny gem

of daylight. They live in depth: not long.
They sell themselves to ruin for a song.

Over But Not Over But Over

All things seem the mention of themselves...
                              —John Ashbery

It's like a stage set, not yet struck, silent
now the show is over. Right where Hamlet
died, the truck dispatcher and the nurse
practitioner in sneakers mill about awhile,

waiting to congratulate their Rosencrantz.
They smile, still elated in the blank-verse
trance. The empty poison cup, put back
by Gertrude's sponsor on the prop-rack,

glows teal in a gel's bright stare, so cold
to see, so hot to feel up there. All smiles,
it's like a movie screen where credits roll
as happy couples shimmy to the aisles.

Once the first reel kills off Jimmy Dean,
the next is blank, or just what I've just seen.

What's So Ugly

Uglier than dark soot on a beaten dog
chained to a dying tree, the misery
of both gone silent in a city fog,
too tired to keep crying, too sad to see

how anything could change at this late date
beyond the windchimes tolling them to sleep.
Ugly like what angry people throw: great
paper drifts of litter, bottles busting, cheap

gifts, broken, obsolete, that failed to cheer
the children they were meant to bribe. I failed
to learn from life, from death, from reading *Lear*
again, the simple formula that's nailed

onto the wall inside me: humility
is strength. I don't learn. That's what's so ugly.

Hot January
For Daniel Kaufman

Beaten by desire, beard whiter every day,
in my apartment like Jonah in the whale,
I read until the books all turn to stone.
Jewish, sober, bitterly divorced
and scared to death of His eternal fist,
I'm dry. Hot January spooks us pale.
I feel my hollow happiness rip wide,
and glossy ravens spread to make
their airborne dash from my disease.
The mild weather's timing terrifies
even as it soothes, until the ancient air
is coppered by the setting Sun again,
and daylight fails, impaled on darkness.
Sex will save me, surely. Never. Now.

She's Gone, But

I guess it's not so bad. I would've had
to give up all my vices, under scrutiny,
and done big shame when next I screwed-up-bad.
My Ego and my Id would stage a mutiny,

and Superego, never very super,
would be overthrown and I'd go wild again.
Or they'd surrender in a silent stupor
so my inner Boss could boss me till I smiled again.

Now there's nobody to change for.
I'm too busted up by grief and self
pity, lately, to bring down *Major
Trends in Jewish Mysticism* off the shelf

and dare learn something new. I look
at love and piety from outside, in a book.

The Meaning of Life Is the Location of the Universe
For my parents

As for life, others lived it before I was born.
Others will live it after I am gone.
Like you, I am living it now.

Until today, this was something I simply knew.
But now it has a body, like a bird,
and the blue fact of it is hovering in front of me.

My grandfather died in a bed between two chairs.
My dad sat at his left and I sat at his right:
only three places to be. One place at a time.

As for life, others lived it before I was born.
Others will live it after I am gone.
I am living it now. Only stories within life
can have meaning. Life as a whole just can't.

The universe can't move. It isn't in a place.
Only positions inside it are somewhere.
Before I'm gone, others will experience youth.
House to house the tracks of them unfurl
the dawn's ephemeral ribbon.

I miss my mother. She had a nightgown
made of silk, that hung deep in the walk-in closet.

When nobody was home, I crept inside
and rubbed the milky hem against my cheek.

Others lived it before I was born.
The meaning of life is the location of the universe.
As for life, I am living it now.

II

Chariot

Lethal bronze twin green wheels roll.
The driver cranes his neck,
pouring his attention down the field.
The team sweats in the yoke and drags it all.

The Sun is hid by hot wind dark with dust,
then red, then gone before the fighting stops.
Both mares are angry, scared, then mad again;
they go; they gather the rest of their spirit and run.

Above the axle of the giant rims, the shaking tiny car
seats two. One rises tugging on the reins, leans over
to the burning eastern yard, blood flashing in the dark.
A tent hit by a torch. Dogs running from a wall of fire.

He pivots frightened, angry, westward, his brother
half unconscious at the right wheel's twisted rail.
The chariot comes on, the night is torn, death rises for them:
both of the chariot's men, and one of its two young horses.

HOMER'S *ILIAD*, BOOK I LINES 1–66*

Anger, sing, Goddess, of Peleus' son Achilles,
Ruinous, that upon the Achaeans wrought agonies myriad,
And threw thus into Hades many heroes' mighty souls;
A prize for dogs it made of them, and supper for the vultures:
The will of Zeus was being fulfilled. From that point
Whereat they first began to stand apart, the pair of them feuding,
Atreus' son the lord of men, and the divine Achilles.
Which God was it then, that threw them together in strife,
To make them fight? The Son of Leto and Zeus,
For He was angry with the king, and up through their encampment
He traversed the army, scattering an horrible disease. And the people
    were dying.
This because Atreus' son had slighted one Chryses, though Apollo's
    very priest.
Close to the swift Achaean ships he had come for to ransom
    his daughter,
Laden with opulent gifts. Bearing in hand woven branches
Of the distant-shooting Apollo, that crowned a golden scepter,
He beseeched all the Achaeans, most of all Atreus' two sons,
That ruled the people: *Atreus' sons, and other armored Achaeans,*
To you may the Gods that have homes on Olympus grant it:
To sack the city of Priam and safely return, arriving at home again.
But give to me my own dear child, and take in the ransom:
Respecting Apollo, the distant-shooting Son of Zeus. Then,
Though all Achaeans else cried out their loud approval, thus

---

*Note that several Homeric terms refer to the Greeks at the Trojan War: Achaeans, Danaans, and Hellenes ("Greeks" is the Roman word for them). Several terms refer to the God Apollo: Phoebus, Smintheus, and Son of Leto and Zeus. The term "sons of Atreus" (Greek *Atreidae*) refers to Agamemnon (high king of the entire Greek force) and his brother Menelaus (whose wife Helen was kidnapped by the Trojan prince Paris, which started the Trojan War).

To reverence the priest, and receive the shining ransom,
Yet Agamemnon son of Atreus was not pleased in his heart,
But sent him away disgracefully, and made a speech of power to him:
Do not, old man, let me catch you beside these hollow ships,
Neither tarrying now nor coming later on, lest your scepter
And the fillets of the God fail to protect you. But return the girl I shall not:
Sooner shall Old Age take her, in our own home far from the land of her fathers
Going back and forth about the loom, and into my bed, to join there.
But go! Nor provoke me further; that will be safer for you.
He spoke thus, and the old man was afraid, and heeded his command.
Silently then, he sought the abundantly murmuring shoreline of Ocean,
And when the old man had gone quite far from the army,
He prayed in earnest to the Lord Apollo, born from Leto of the lovely hair:
Hear me, Lord of the silver bow, Who walk about divine Chryse and Cilla,
And reign in power over Tenedos: O Smintheus, if ever I covered with a lovely roof
Your temple, or if indeed I ever burnt for You slices of fat and cutlets
From the thighs of bulls or of goats, fulfill for me this wish: let the Danaans
Pay for my tears with Your arrows. Thus he spoke praying, and Phoebus Apollo
Heard him, and stepped from the head of the mountain Olympus, rage in His heart;
He bore on His shoulders the bow and a sheathed quiver; as He moved
In His anger, the arrows clanged on His shoulders. And He came on like the night.
He had been seated away from the ships, but then into the heart of the camp
He let fly a missile, and the noise of the silver bow became terrifying,
Taking first the mules, and then the shining dogs, and next the men themselves
He attacked with the bitter arrows, and shot them. Always there burned
The close-crowded pyres of corpses. Nine days the arrows of the God
Flew up the army. Achilles the tenth day called to Assembly the people:

Hera the white-armed Goddess had into his spirit suggested the notion:
For She was distressed for the Hellenes, as She saw them perishing.
And so when they had gathered together, among them there stood up
Achilles of the swift feet, and spoke to them: *Atreus' son, now*
I believe we shall be driven back, and return again homeward, if indeed
We should escape death, if war and plague alike are to beset the Achaeans.
But come, let us ask some mantis or holy man, or even
Some interpreter of Dreams—for a Dream, too, comes from Zeus—
Who might tell us of Phoebus Apollo's anger: whether He holds us blameworthy
For lack of a huge cattle-sacrifice, prayer, or the smoke of a lamb or perfect goat,
If He should be willing to trade for this, and ward-off from us the plague.

Homer's *Iliad*, Book IV lines 1–42

Gathered together by Zeus, all the reclining Gods
Lay on the golden floor. Before Them, Mistress Hebe
Poured Their nectar. Into the golden floor They gazed then,
Down on the city of Troy They bartered away in pledges.
Kronos' Son made trial of Hera, baiting Her, quarreling;
In these devious words with sidelong glance He addressed Her:
Two defenders has Menelaus among the Immortals:
Argive Hera, and the Protector, deathless Athena—
Nevertheless, the two of Them sitting apart are enjoying
Watching; while Aphrodite, Whose care is but laughter, always
Goes to the side of Her darling and keeps him from ruin;
Even now She has saved him again, who expected to perish.
Victory, all the same, has fallen to harsh Menelaus.
What shall We say—whatever the outcome of all these deeds—
Shall We bestir the disasters of battle and raise up war
Hateful and deadly, or throw between them a dear understanding?
If, somehow, this peace has become what all of You wish for,
Finding it sweet and dear to Your hearts, let the city of Priam
Thrive and be lived in, and let Menelaus take his Helen.
Thus He spoke, and They muttered against Him—Athena and Hera.
Near one another the Goddesses sat and devised, for the Trojans,
Evils. Athena was stubborn and would not speak one word.
She was enraged at Zeus Her Father, and seized by anger.
But Hera spoke. Her breast could not contain Her fury:
Mightiest one, Son of Kronos, what sort of word have You spoken?
Why would You make idle and vain the pains I have taken,
My sweat, and the sweat of My toiling horses that labored to summon
Soldiers to bring the destruction of Priam, himself and his children?
Do it! But not quite all the remainder will shout Their approval.
Angry with Hera, Zeus of the gathering clouds spoke back:

Darling, what evils have Priam and Priam's children done You,
Making You vehement, eagerly yearning to ravage the citadel,
Ilium's well-built city to break into pieces forever?
If You went through the gates and the high-built walls of the entrance,
Eating Priam's children raw, devouring Priam,
And other Trojans: that would appease You, and cure Your anger.
Do what You like: let not this small quarrel between Us
Grow to a great one, and sunder Us further.
See that You keep in Your heart this word that I give You:
When in the future I yearn to destroy some city You cherish
Wherein mortals dwell who are dear to You, do not object to it:
Waste no time opposing My rage, and let Me destroy them.

The Sirens

1.

It is not right that Circe's words
Should enter my ears only, secret
From you men who pull your hearts out
At my oars, shot at, beaten brainless
By the Cyclops I provoked, driven
By Poseidon's stormy hate: so,
I will tell you: we will come soon
To the island of the sister Sirens
Standing in their flowery meadow
Where about their feet lie violets,
Lilies, lemongrass, teeth and fingers
Of the sailors who, before us, landed
On their dreamy strand for music.
There lay they long repenting of it, yet
From inside that music they could not
Go back, and as this music built
A world of towers, stairways, halls
Inside their minds, their bellies cried
For food until their bodies failed. So
With these bolts of braided cord
Must you now tie me to the ship
Lashing my trunk to the olive pole
Whereon our sail waits for the wind.
That is not all: Circe instructs me,
I must fill your ears with beeswax now
Lest when our black ship slides beside
Their pretty field, the sweet airs pour
From their twin throats into you all

To steal away your wits forever,
With all of Ithaca, children, wives,
Possessions, friends, all memories of love
Dissolved into their music like one wave
Into the next, sailor after sailor, life
Collapsing into story, persons into memory,
Memory into endless dream, unspeakable.

2.

Disappointing somehow, though correct
About my record in the War, my kills,
My wounds, my old scar from the forest.
Their song is greater than my tale of pain,
Their voices, feminine, more searching
Than these dying ships, that chase
The Pole Star on his speeding way.
Most of what they sang was true: Dolon
I murdered; I stole the great black ram
From Polyphemus, and his eyesight.
Yes, I spend my men like money. Yes
I killed the stag, that fed my starving men
Whose friends were eaten raw by giants.
Mine was the scheme for the hollow horse,
And when I found myself an isolate,
Hemmed in by the Lykian ranks,
I fought my way to No Man's land
Between the armies, and my name
For some time vanished from my mind
Though all up and down I searched for it.
All this happened as the Sirens said.
But then they pushed their music on, in
Deeper into my heart's ear, into the dark
Below my mind, so that my blood

Was poisoned and perfumed with this
Mazy melody and harmony mingling.
While this enthralling chord of fire
Was weaving in their voices on the air
Twin streams of endless breath
Above the meadow and the waves,
I listened to the music and became a slave.
I saw the arms of Eurylochos rowing,
I saw beside him the others rowing along,
And the island moved away, and the twin
Sisters singing receded so swiftly, so
Suddenly did the spell break that I heard
My own voice still shouting *untie me*
Untie me untie me though meanwhile
Inside I was praying to Athena that we
Get clear of that island of the two Sirens.

SAVING AJAX

Achilles is dead. Who will win the honor of his arms?
His breastplate, helmet, greaves, his famous shield—
what will decide their fate among the kings?
A vote of Trojan prisoners: who hurt them most?
A vote among the Greeks? Decree from Agamemnon?
Ajax and Odysseus the champions vie for the prize.

How should any witness intervene? Dig
back, for poor dumb mighty Ajax, back
behind the old disaster of his words,
before he broke the back of his own life
in headlong folly speaking broad insolence
to Her, the Grey-Eyed Goddess, Daughter
of Zeus: Pallas Athene Parthene.*

Reader, take up this hopeless labor:
slip the rules of nature, and play
truant from the schoolhouse of this world:
save him. Warn him. Train him to the holy,
humbly to receive its gift of strength,
nor take for granted one God-granted breath,
but reach, with that one-half-of-mind that can,
into the liquid dark of fear, to find love's root.

---

*Pronounced *Pal*-las Ah-*thay*-nay *Par*-thay-nay.

Open his heart's eye, in reverence bittersweet,
hard bliss, and holy gratitude. Help Ajax
to bow down before the God, to love
his Mother and be loved, discover
new experience in rapt, suspended
thought, and bring to windy Troy
a life uncracked by curse or blunder.

Polonius' Lament

Ophelia, I am thy father's spirit, doomed for a certain term
To starve in deserts of the mind, unsaying word by word
The decades of my rant, my heartless jibes and carping.
Guided by the shades of ancient sinners, I repent me now
Of all my spying, lying, sniveling pride, my busy seeking;
I turn about, to pledge in terms most absolute and evergreen
Full humble restitution of my undelivered love, together
With those blessings I poured out upon your brother's head,
From yesterday and my death until the end of time, *Amen*.
You that I neglected, used, and traded as I would a calf,
You that I destroyed, your heart upon my broken horn,
My bitter, petty prudence, my infected brain of envy! O
Ophelia, I repent me all my sins against thee and revere
Your holy love that frightened me. Your royal lover
Loves you after all: I was wrong, and died of it.
After Earth and flesh, in Hades all we sorry shades
Disport us in such business as we knew in life, but now,
O daughter whom I burden with these secrets, oh now
We fast in fires! We do not consume, and though we burn,
Yet are we not consumed. I come to beg forgiveness.
The wind behind me shakes the reeds on Lethe wharf.
Forgive me, forgive me, forgive me. Lady, forget me.

Barnardine

A minor character in Shakespeare's *Measure for Measure*,
the source of the lines in italics, speaks to the audience:

A pox on your throats! Who makes that noise there?
What are you? I hear the breath of you, new visitors.
I see your eyes, rings, buttons: tiny flashes in the dark.
I know you're there. When I get soused you come
Invisible to stare at me; you clean and dry,
Me drunk and rotting in my filthy cell, alone
But for Abhorson's jangling keys; cats and mice;
The drabs and thieves and bawds and heretics
I never meet, that come and go, or come and die
On seven floors of dust and misery below me.
I know you haunt me from your stupid towns
Ages hence, your English watered down like this
White gruel for breakfast, lunch, and supper.
You ticket-holders patronize the past
One hour a month, to think on us dead people
With your easy grace, and shoe your horses
With old iron of our blood, oblivious and gay.
Each of you a moth, a mayfly, guests of Earth
Who swagger to Her table like you own the place.
Well, listen, spirits of posterity: my piss
Is in your veins, my spit diffused into your wine
Like Julius Caesar's guts in my own Rhenish.
All you proud, sweet ladies, all you learned men,
You're made of bits of me. I'm more free than you,
Jailed up as I am in *Measure for Measure*, three hour
Slab of orphaned life that floats like driftwood
On the face of history, buoyant, undissolved.

I will not consent to die this day, that's certain:
It's the only day I have. It has me, and I have it
Always. My bottle's never empty. Nine years?
I'm in here since 1604. No news from Abhorson
But *the warrant's come*; no outside
Waiting to receive me from the cell, the ward,
The drink, the script, the body: when the Duke
Delivers me from bondage, all things end again.
But then an instant later they again begin.
So I am drunk, guilty of a pair of murders,
Gravel-hearted, bored, no home, no shame.
My seven lines and I are still the same.

Paradise and Hell Lost

Milton's Satan stood on a twisted spire of driftwood
At the shore of Heaven's unnamed sea, where crabs
Scrambled deaf in their archaic shells; otters tumbled
Glad among the mild troughs swept forever inland
To the strand of the unbounded East. Milton's Satan
Had a pocketful of Paxil for the week. It made him fat,
But kept him from the open jaws, the jet black throat,
The noisome guts of the Abyss. Instead, the seagulls
Keening in the breeze, as overhead Arcturus burned
Third-brightest in the sky, red giant mired in planets.
Instead of Hell, eternal April by the shoals, wild oats
Waving in the dunes, and myriad pearls half buried
In the sand, greened by the glow of lambent algae.
He likes it here in Limbo, on parole a billion years.
Milton's Satan sat out the Jurassic, playing to a draw
Ten thousand of the fallen angels he had led astray
That now sat pensive in their plastic folding chairs
Across the chessboards, playing black to Milton's
Satan's white. Generations of the tortoise
Live and die between the moves; glaciers rise
Between the castling and the captured Queen.
Octagonal Lamictal made him stable but lethargic;
Depakote was hard to get aroused with; Prozac
Wouldn't work unless he never took another sip
Of wine or babies' blood again; and cannabis
Just kept him up all night, idly swinging back
And forth, back and forth, his hammock pinned
Across the two horns of the Moon, his body
Massive as an Alp, supine in the sagging mesh.
No wagers rode the outcome of that stalemate,

No tournament, no prize, and brimming horns,
Foam-headed, of O'Doul's non-alcoholic brew
Lay yet untouched about the dais where the skim
Milk glowed blue-white beside the fat-free cakes.
Now and then the ensigns or lieutenants took a break,
Expending dental dams and condoms, if they could.
As one of God's lost pods of pilot whales approached
That starry shore, the Artist Formerly Known As Lucifer
Turned to the largest male and introduced himself.
"*Hello,*" he said, "*I'm Milton's Satan.*" But the pale
Amorphous mist had wrapped his words, and now
The train of thought was broken, and he could not
Remember whether he had only thought, or spoken.

Satan's Moods

Affluent, Satan bites his nails at home,
planning a giant party for himself
with go-go girls and go-go boys galore,
and a great brass band, and punch in goblets.

Between his heart and spleen, his envy rides.
What is love? He gave up, but it didn't help.
Flashes of joy when glasses break, or bones
of other people, or the arms of stone

god statues that will not be whole again.
Flashes of peace when doctors burn alive.
Exactly how he got here is a mystery
the centuries can't solve. What do they mean,

those dreams of falling through the clouds?
Why so angry? And why these tears again?

Faustus

As you walk into your room, behold
a devil in a Hefner jacket smoking
in your favorite chair. Mephistopheles
offers you two boxes of your own cigars
and starts his pitch: I'll give you twenty-four
years of magical power (for your soul,
of course) with all the inches, gold
and genius you could possibly desire.
You think about it. I'll fix the fire.

The Seven Deadly Sins

Envy is the rainbow, iridescent on the stagnant pool,
gazing up all morning at his brother in the sky.
Pride, a dog that says: "I." And then, "am the Messiah."
Lust is the body's endless blank book, burning in the dark.
Avarice, a well dug down to China, dry as dust.
Wrath, the pit bull's granite skull, split by the rail spike.
Sloth, that flooded creek where all my papers fell.
Vanity, one iridescent blue-green beetle in the dirt.

Mania

I see men as trees, walking.
                    —Mark 8:24

My sentient light, that was extinct, has come back on.
I rise toward the summit of the night, drilling through the dark.
Now like the blind man of Mark 8:24, I'm given other vision.
I peer between the speaking roots of trees below the water table,
scan the flooded grave-shafts in the hills; touch Dante's skull.
Inside an airless tomb I mount the skeletal roan gelding of the King.

Numbers, fresh from hidden currents of the sea, thrive in my mouth.
They glaze my spirit's folded surface, a single wet square mile.
Without a word, I know the inmost thoughts of each and all;
discern the constellations in July's blue afternoon. I overhear
dolphins sing, a hemisphere away, the shapes of tall cold
eddies in their midst, that stir green nebulae of motes.

Living jellies, undiscovered in the deepest sea,
range up and down my ken. I walk straight on
through checkpoints like a ghostly dog; I'm
undetectable. I see through miles of concrete.
Ordnance does no harm; bullets cross the region of me
unimpeded. I live on, despite the snipers' aim.
I am here as if I had a body, but no body's here.

Dawn and evening come and go. Days, and weeks of days,
I watch: new empires' every move, at each other's throats.
Great telescopes named Keck, Mt. Wilson, Palomar and Lick,
the Very Large Array. The sea-slug's neural network: green, electric.
And as my spectral arm extends directly through a yard of books,
the pages yield their essence to my hand, until I'm found.

The Earth Was without Form, and Void

People say that God is the greatest of beings. But I say that God is as far above Being and Nothingness as the sun is above a fly.
—Meister Eckhart

Time is a number, moving itself.
—Aristotle

No world, nor any screen
to frame the circle of the sight
where white would yield to white.
Vacant hours of the night
escape their days, and roll
away from fiction and the truth.
Air, and no one there to breathe.
Waves cross the blank mind of the sea.
Space blows the stars along the dark.
Time holds a flaming stone.
Infinity walks naked in a circle.

"Strong Thunderstorms Result in Deaths of Two"
—*New York Times*, August 9th, 1992

Two people working, maybe in love.
Instep arches on the ladder rounds,
arms raised to drape the giant leaves
over the rafter-beams, bright laughter.

Not the worst way to die: hanging tobacco
in a barn, when the roof of the world breaks
down into the ceiling with white blood
straight out of God's right arm, pure light.

Rebuffed by the universe, stung in the mouth
by Earth, both faces vaporized,
spines and futures forfeit to the air.
I.D. by dentition in the burned-out loft.

Absolutely sudden. Totally destroyed.
After the lightning, nobody is there.

III

The Late Beach
For Nandi Johannes

Look what recent trash and trinkets
circle the bent litterbasket, cast
wide of it, into the shade beside it
on the sand. Here's a rubber band.
The handle from a radio.
Leaflets go, hover, wait, fall off
the wind's convex invisible face;
dissolve in the loud cold waves.
Gulls raise the chalice of the breeze.
Terns keen in layers of the air.
A green rag rides the tide.
Cups and matches, coins,
pistachios that would not open,
poison clams, closed and broken,
and a broken pencil buried in the sand.

1994

The Ride

This late in the ride
the sun is nearly gone
though light enough remains
to show the fields:
wild grass, with endless water
ending in sudden hills beyond,
and past them, wild grass again
teeming in the blue obscure.
Now houses light themselves
behind the trees,
disclose the brief interiors
and disappear
as hills and darkness
open to the train.

1989

GLOVES (or, Night's Hand)

Into the left glove's open lips
Place the cone of fingertips.
Each finger will seek out
One tiny leather mouth.
So should this living hand replace
Night's hand of empty space.

Revolving Door

The sound of the revolving door
is like the sound of the sea,
washing people in and out
the building (like pale crabs,
borne helpless on the tide)
till night falls and they lock it.
He who was in, is out. She
who was out is in, because
the panels spin, until she
stops the turns and blocks it.
The wall makes a boundary,
and the door mocks it.

Pencil Sharpener

Housed in a bulbous shell,
a tube of grey-black razor blades
waits in the dark for the next one.
Pencils come and go, asleep,
unwilling and incapable of work.
They leave alive and terrified,
as sharp as new-made nails.
Churned by hand, or motorized,
gears shave away the jaded past,
lay bare the graphite in the wood
and leave for trash the shed skins
of long dead pine, its tendrils
corkscrewed in the vestibule.
Work now, tortured pencil,
deaf instrument worn down
to uselessness and back
by work, its mark brought
back from blank to black.

Housework
For Kama Einhorn

I consider as I sweep the floor
the broad back of a sleepy whale
and I am grooming her skin
with the great corn brush
of my mighty little broom.

I consider as I make the bed
the spread sails of a clipper
in a pristine bay long ago
while the belly of my sheet
descends from near the ceiling.

I consider as I do the dishes
long cold fishes of the deep,
ancient, nimble, sentient
in the dark one mile below
the white spume of the storm.

2017

Homage to Billy Collins

Billy Collins could not be here this morning,
so I am writing his poem for him.
In it, a dog sleeps beside a tree,
while that little girl from the painting
by de Chirico chases her almost silent hoop.
And you are there, and from his window
Billy Collins sees you and, too busy writing
a much better poem than this one,
wonders for a moment: how you got here,
and why you are wearing his bathrobe.

Casper the Friendly Ghost

Casper alights on a statue in the dawn.
He is the Messiah: deny it and be damned.
O ectoplasmic tyke, have mercy on us.
Killed by middle-management,
Casper has forsworn revenge.
Paradise claims his marshmallow bosom.
The onus of his karma is dispersed.
Henceforth the milky Bodhisattva
joins us for our fragile welfare,
and to his spectral ministry
the better part of us
remains oblivious:
grownups don't understand,
but children love him the most:
Casper the F. Ghost.

Oscar the Grouch Crosses the Pacific Garbage Patch

A floating wasteland frowning at the sky,
sprawling great as Texas on the toxic sea,
threaded by the needle of his tiny transit:
as he goes, the gap of his brief wake is closed.
The noise of the garbage is thick yet soft,
mingling news from plastic, wood, and air,
as all those surfaces yield senseless sound
shaped by chaos to the long white noise.
To Oscar this is music, glorious, enough
to saturate his spirit with its secret song.
No living soul for miles. As Oscar swims,
He sings a haunting version of his own
theme: "I Love Trash," now in a minor key
and slowed down to the tempo of a dirge.
His soul is bared: thrilled, and very scared.

Livestock in the Eisenhower Years

Aw nerts / One of them might say, *this guy's too much for me.*
                                              —John Ashbery

Fabian! Holsteins dump their methane up to Sputnik.
Edsel! Corvair! Ten thousand thousand chickens piss
ammonia up the air, to rip the sky right out from over
that coiffed n' kerchieffed head: the one and only
Lucille Ball, who snacks on porkloin won from half-ton
sows that coat the wall with blood on slaughterday.
Bowels blasting all year round, they melt the metal
doorknobs of their pens. The five-pound plastic
post-war phone where romance was transduced from sound
to numbers, back to sound, rerouted through the soul and back
into the phone, cooks in the utter darkness of the landfill
where the days ferment. Pep-rally. Cookout. Destiny.

Noah

The God could not be bothered to exist,
yet He saw fit, in His good goodness,
to hassle Noah with a crazy plan
to build an ark against the coming flood.
The signals came in droves at first:
messages in junk, or patterns in the ashtray,
napkins, oatmeal, shadows of the trees
on a bar's brick whitewashed wall.
It all said *BUILD A GIANT BOAT* so he did.
He built it out of Styrofoam and tape,
green plastic empties, newspaper and twine,
packets of soy sauce, plastic knives.
It filled the whole backyard. Ordinary eyes,
the dead eyes of the damned, saw nothing
but a twenty-two foot heap of trash.
But the Ark was all to Noah; deep and tall,
broad, spacious and serene, austere,
seaworthy. Here a pair of apes
would sleep, and here, two cheetahs
lulled by one another's warmth
and breath and rumbling purr, would wait
the slow duration of the forty days; here,
the male iguana and the female could repose
along the corrugated cardboard slabs.
No breeding couple of rhinoceros around,
he had to settle for a picture from a magazine
he stapled to a pizza box. The flood would come,
the waves would sweep it all away: strip malls,
billboards, cars, until the ark alone remain
drifting someday on an almost windless sea.

The Golem

One day the Rebbe made a Golem.
The riverbank is all clay, miles long.
Down beside the rushing stream
gingerly stepped the bearded Jew,
his canvas bag of sculptor's tools
slung across his pious shoulders' shawl.
In his hands, twin pails to fill
and empty on the wagon's floor.
The Rebbe loaded up the cart all day
with all the clay his horse could bear
homeward to the cellar, with its tin chute
down which rolled one hundred four
clay cores into position by the door.
Secret now, they float in air, held there
by the Rebbe's mind of humble power.
Out now come his tools, some long
steel instruments, some wood
with loops of rigid wire. He set to work,
and carved the heap into a giant man,
making his trunk of ribs, twelve pair;
his mighty legs; two feet; a genital;
until the time of truth, penultimate,
when down into the man's blank front
the Rebbe leaned, and with his old hands
made the Golem's very face.
Magical he moved, conjuring by God
the Holy Name he dared inscribe
upon the broad wet forehead of the Golem.
So with his prayers, contentment
with his lot, surrender, detachment

and attachment both in moderation,
meditation, holy charms and psalms
in haunting melodies, sung with shaking,
he pierced a pinhole into Heaven
through which a free and curious soul
swam willing into the solid empty Golem,
who blinked. He blinked again. His nostrils
flared, and for the first time breathed a breath.
Sat up, and shook his head. Smiled. Moved
to rest his chin upon his knee, and wondered
what would be the mission, for which he, a Golem,
had been summoned into life, with holy labor,
and with elements of Earth and Heaven?

Music

Just waves in the world,
music is a state of the air.
Just warm and moving meat,
the body is a state of the soil.

Compressions of the wind,
or of the still air that waits.
Vibrations of three tiny bones
inside the ear, combine
to conjure sound from math.
Music is messages inscrutable.
It is an aimless summons.

Heed! it says. Heed what?
Come! it urges. Where?
Remember! Which thing?
Yearn! And *that*, we can do.

HUGO WOLF (Austrian Slovenian composer, 1860–1903)

King and beggar, wretch and lord of joy,
your losing war with germs from Satan
cost you every dignity and hope.
Down through the hole of death your arm

reached to touch the poets of the past,
and took up lyrics from the silent dark:
Goethe, Mörike, Eichendorff
live again because you heard their pain

and set their poems to the airs of God.
A baby first, then *maestro*, then again
an infant: fecal smearing in a padded cell.
No mercy from the poisons of your blood,

no second breast to bring you back to life.
Time, space, and sanity divide us now.

AAFJE HEYNIS (Dutch contralto, 1924–2015)

Silk ribbons on the air. A spinning ball
of water, hovering before you. A crown
of floating silk above your head. These
the sort of thing we say, now you are

gone, to touch the life of what
your voice was like. Recordings
show to anyone with ears to hear you
is to bend one's inner body down,

humbly to that river of the liquid light
from which the saints, Augustine
and Monica his mother, drank deep
just after Rome was sacked and burned.

Your spirit sips at the water's edge,
shoulder to shoulder with us all.

MARIA CALLAS (Greek American soprano, 1923–1977)
For David Benesty

Consciousness is not a tiny bit of the world stuck on the rest of it. It is the inside of the whole world.

—Owen Barfield

In dreams you rolled an icy stone
up to a jagged peak; met very Death
walking toward you on the wind,
trailing spectral robes, his violin
calling you to join him on his way.
Awake, you joined him on his way.
Along one strip of space-time still
your "Norma" shimmers in the past.
Your breath made demons chase
the sound's expanding sphere: a voice
to span the sweet interior of space.

IV

Wedding Wagon

I read about a wagon in a field,
long overturned, and full of faded grass.
It burned all night, when lightning shot the wheel.
It vanished in the smoke, into the past

where still it rolls contented down a lane
of flowers, on the way to weddings, joy
and love and youth all riding through the rain—
till money made a soldier of the boy,

and time put bitter ruth into the girl.
I heard about the wagon in the field
that burned all night, when that part of the world
was lit by lightning and the fire peeled

the paint, and curled the boards, and drove it back
into the time when it was not yet black.

Problem Solving
For John P. Sullivan

Who was still in there, when the story ended?
Who got out in time? How did this outcome
come about? Why couldn't it stay suspended
till someone clever learned to climb some

paper mountain of arcane equations,
stand elated and exhausted on the peak,
and tell the world what works on all occasions
to unite the forces: gravity, electro-weak,

and strong? How is it we all have to die
without solutions to our species' most
urgent burning questions: what is time? Why
does light exist at one speed only? Post-

apocalyptic scratches on a burned-out car.
Your next meal. Mine. That tree. That star.

Harmless

My harmless poem is touching this paper in your hand.
Both are dying but the poem has another body waiting
on the dark side of the Moon. You have a wooden box
waiting, and a song, and a carousel of suits and dresses,
black, with relatives and friends inside, milling about
among bronze urns of purple flowers below a ceiling fan.
Hear their heartbeats, hear them coughing in the hallway.
Watch the angelic cavalry traverse their fantasy of you.
Hear silver hoofbeats ring the pediments of Heaven
as your soul arrives among the terraced choirs of light.
What will you sing? A billion of the hovering Saved
heave their radiant breasts in mounting harmonies,
but you hear absolutely nothing. They ignore you.
They are pouring their attention down a central hole.

THE ROUND SQUARE (or, Manifesto of the Left Hemisphere)

Why is there a world at all? Guy stands up and says,
God made the world, and as for who made God, well,
That's just a mystery beyond us. Woman says,
A round square is not a mystery beyond us;
It's neither real nor imaginary; it's not a concept,
Not an object, neither nothing nor an Entity.
He says, that's what I'm saying, it's incomprehensible.
No, she says, there's nothing there to comprehend.
He says, of course there is, and we both know it.
She says, you're bobbing for apples of relief, love,
And immortality, and along comes a word. The word
Is a noun and pretty soon you're making it the subject
Of a world of verbs, and then the miracles begin. She says,
God is logic's corpse, a wound in reason, grammar's empty skin.

2006

Tyrannosaurus Rex

I am *Tyrannosaurus Rex*.
Hunger is my crown.
The sun assails me.
My own blood is fire!
I need no sun.
My scales of gilded green
absorb the hateful light.
I swelter daylong in the ferns
until I smell another meal,
Diplodocus, walk down
-river in a pod of nine.
My saliva flows, infected, toxic.
I tremble and my life
explodes to motion and I kill one.
My skin crawls, slick sheath
of flawless tiny tiles. Ripples.
Without the flesh of others,
my own flesh will die.
Twice I almost died.
In my tiny mind,
a pilot light was kindled
partway down
my lifetime's shapeless span.
Nowhere near words,
I note the coming dawn;
from utter darkness
I have almost reached
the shore of sentience,
its distant glimmer.
Ankle-deep in Lethe,

I ply the ferns
on my earth-shaking legs
and wend my way
to blood, meat,
the marvel of my thunder-scream
astonishingly loud. I break
Diplodocus in two,
and eat his liver
in the rain.
Tiny cymbals
clang and quiver
in my little brain.

The Razorback

Our wagon-train departed in the fall.
We tracked the Razorback, magnificent,
a granite boar ungodly huge and black,
a waving comb of bristles on its rock of a back.
We lost decades in the forest. We found dung
and tracks, broad troughs of broken branches.
The Razorback came at us like a living wall.
My friends he gored to death, but I survived.
We broke him in the ashes of his home.

Eohippus: "Dawn Horse"

Nowhere now, archaic Spain's
goat-sized proto-horse,
Eohippus, innocent and gone,
still gone a million years from Tuesday:

yet they will still be walking, eating,
getting killed, back there in the Eocene.
Lions of their mornings brought
dismemberment, not shame.

Three million individuals
stride between parentheses,
mate and run and dream between
that wide-divided pair of hands:

the open early hand from which
the species gradually springs,
and the later fist of minutes when
the last of them collapses in a tar pit.

Giant Extinct Camel

Some other camel will have had sex with you, O
Giant Extinct Camel. As good as that felt,
it was so long ago your bones have been
dispersed in three dimensions in the dark
below the tar, and what I'm standing at
and talking to is just a statue made of camel bones
from heaps of individuals. Maybe you and she
are both a part of it—her leg, your skull,
the toes of someone seven generations back.
You're so gone, this sculpture isn't even
where you are, nor where you're missing from.

Dying Bee

Have you seen the dying bee? It moves,
but not toward anything. It's still
absorbing air and light still fires off
the cells that line the backs of its enormous eyes.
Still there, the two antennae seem to work,
but after this, there's nothing to detect
except a million empty pores of concrete
sidewalk where it shoves its flat back legs
behind it like a tortoise. Wings
that saw the world now stop.
Mandibles, that drank the sun
from fifteen thousand flowers,
on final lovely unreal pollen close.

The Death of the Fly

Through the frog's throat the fly goes buzzing madly,
wet wings folded useless in the foreign slime,
and trauma's telescoped equations slow down
time into a million razor-thin splinters of panic
moving through the dying bug still struggling
to be free, or dead, but not enveloped any more
in acid darkness burning all over, violated.
The fly's complicated body fails. Its spirit,
simple, shakes once and sifts its way outside.

Fly Killing

I'll get you, housefly, for all my sins and yours.
This rolled up magazine, my will, my iron hand,
Will blast the cream of your mysterious insides
To the wall. My house is not for you. I'll kill
The sight and sound of you; I'll use the accident
Of me, my middle age, my arc and overthrow.
Come here: I'll take our ego down in one great blow;
Reduce us to a smear; break open your absurd religion,
Noise; your love of shit; the parasites you propagate;
The fat white lie inside the craven heart of each of us.
Keep it up, bug. You're free to go, but you don't.
Nobody forced you to move in and mock me.
Now that you know we are one, do as you choose.
But here's my version of you, with the news.

Yeast in a Vat: A Parable

The yeast in a vat
of sweet grape juice
eat up all the sugar,
using it to build more yeast
with toxic alcohol as waste
till there's no sugar left:
just when the thriving yeast in their billions hit their highest peak
    of population,
awash in alcohol
with nothing to eat.
We are the yeast.
Earth is the vat.
It is not our fault.

Fido

Under the iron wagon of the past
roll the exceptional bone and ball
irretrievably shoved up oblivion.
My name means "I believe," but
I'm all finished now. Tonight
I'm cold by the telephone pole;
skewered by fever, I'm still outside
pining for my great pink rubber ball,
my cow-bone trailing ragged ligaments.
Without you I'm rain and vapor,
pouring through the chain-link fence,
heartsick for the day that's gone:
the fatted summer where I raced the sun,
still young, still chasing that sidereal car.

Counterfactual

Zeus animates the Trojan Horse, which runs away
across the plains of Troy as, in its hollow belly,
cruel embittered soldiers are digested into slime.

Teen Hitler, by a thunderbolt, is cored like a pear.
Baby Stalin's bladder is turned suddenly to stone.

Up swims Christ from fiction, climbs out
real from the mosaic emblem in the floor
at CIA. By His light are the bones exposed
of pimps and bag-men in their secret halls.

A wild sleet of molten gold and silver rainfall
perforates the screaming heads of Pilate's men,
and Jesus dies an old man in his bed.

The opposite of hope is not despair,
it is the wish for freedom in the past long gone:
the unaborted second term of RFK,
the Yorkist claim triumphant in the field,
Arbenz, Lumumba, Mossadeq,* alive
and signing legislation with a Dodo-feather pen.

I am falling through the story of my life, into the ground.
Catch me, angels of the midnight sun, that rises in the West.
I open *Genesis*, just checking if it's changed at all.
I take my pills and pray to Ingersoll.**

---

*Democratically elected Presidents of Guatemala, Congo, and Iran, all deposed by CIA.
**Robert G. Ingersoll (1833–1899), famous atheist pamphleteer.

BLUEBERRY SWIRL (or, Privilege)

The new flavor is vanilla blueberry swirl.
It's very creamy—you can really taste
that hint of pepper good vanilla brings.
The berries are enormous and I love
the way the fruit picks up those faint
notes of coffee and of cinnamon. But
I am not enjoying it because I know
Felix Rodriguez and Ovando Candia
cut off both of Che Guevara's hands.

Large Big Jumbo

LBJ, you often took a shit in the presence of a U.S. Senator.
You often told the gentleman from Michigan, or some other one
to swim with you, and you swam nude and they cringed and you smiled.
You sold the world from under everyone and made
sad faces in the mirror when it came back broke.

Richard Nixon at Bosworth Field (1485/1974)
For Peter Dale Scott

My kingdom for a horse, a Pegasus to carry me across
The waves from California to Hanoi, higher than my helicopters,
That from her bare back I might cast down through the clouds
My soul-destroying iron spear into the enemy myself.

My kingdom for a slice of pumpkin pie on china in her kitchen,
My mother, whose bliss outshines the sphere of Saturn as,
Above the stars, she passes her immortal days beside the Virgin
On her throne, in robes of gingham; holds in her left hand
    a silver scepter;
In her right, a wicker picnic basket filled with thin ham sandwiches.

My kingdom for one of those loudspeaker cars, rigged with bullhorns,
That I might drive it through Chicago, Dallas, and D.C., its fat Bakelite
Microphone an apple in my trembling hand, the coiled cord pulled taut.
I'd speak again the words I spoke a million years ago into the
    live machine,
The words whose ghost became the 18 Minute Gap, that spouting hiss
Of Moby-Dick, that Siren's aria, eternal music of the spheres,
Hidden like the stars at noon, or like the skeletons my namesake made
Of those two princelings born between my Lord of Gloucester
    and the crown,
Who bled to death beneath their uncle's knife. Both dead boys
    he dragged
Into the closet underneath the stairs below the Tower's Chapel,
Undiscovered for three hundred years and then sequestered in an urn.

My kingdom for a pint of blood, to raise the voice my death made mute,
A pint of blood to feed my homeless shade that loiters in the lobby
Of the Jefferson Memorial, the Mall, the hot coals of the pretzel cart
Whose smoke stings gently in the carriage horses' blinkered eyes.
My ghost looks out from inside giant Lincoln's giant face of
    Colorado marble:
I can see for miles: the frozen grass, plastic bags entangled in
    a million trees,
McDonald's orphaned Styrofoam adrift across the Lower 48,
    dioxin, DDT,
Mount Arlington's white crosses "finite but unbounded"
    like the universe.
If only I could speak, I'd tell you all what words I let escape
The threshold of my teeth into the tape, that day the Devil
Came to Washington, and took possession of my tongue.
You would be grateful I erased it all—the story of your ruin:
how my cold demons in the CIA, my *Mafiosi*, my *Exilios*,
Broke into that hotel to steal the future, and ten years earlier,
They did it: killed the President. Injected me and Lyndon
With the cold black bile of God.

1865

Murder at the Ford and then
the ruined weeks drift out
in starless cold, pitch black.

Soon, green fiddleheads breach
the ashen carpet of the valley.

Dead locomotives come apart,
returning piecemeal to the furnace.

Crowds released from prison,
hospital, and camp, disperse

as when the sudden hail
destroys the beehive:
there, the dead queen.

Here, her aimless drones
and broken soldiers.

One spreading disk
of honey on the ground.

www.ingramcontent.com/pod-product-compliance
Lightning Source LLC
Chambersburg PA
CBHW052200110526
44591CB00012B/2024